EDENTU D. OROSO

Richer Than Pride (A Collection Of Poems)

An Ode To Womanhood

First published by Melodicrose Publishing 2019

Copyright © 2019 by Edentu D. Oroso

All rights reserved. No part of this publication may be reproduced, stored or transmitted in any form or by any means, electronic, mechanical, photocopying, recording, scanning, or otherwise without written permission from the publisher. It is illegal to copy this book, post it to a website, or distribute it by any other means without permission.

First edition

*This book was professionally typeset on Reedsy.
Find out more at reedsy.com*

Dedication
For Princess Timiebi Edentu,
(Whose coming brought sunshine into my life!)

Contents

Acknowledgement iv
Praise For Richer Than Pride v

I Womanhood

Mother 3
Richer Than Pride (An Ode To Womanhood) 5
Joy Is A Vaulted Song 7
Widowhood 9
The Veil 11
The Girl Child 13
Corpse Of An Old Woman 15

II Rhythms Of Life

Life 21
Butterfly 24
Voice Of The Earth 26
Phoenix 28
Water Dialogue 30
Iroko 32
Circumstance 35
Morning Dew 37
Song Of A Butterfly 39
Water 41
I Have Overcome 43

Wisdom Lane	45
Fierce Sickle	47
The Edge Of Silence	49
Celestial Saucer	51
Once Upon A River Benue	53
The Rain	55
Poverty	57
Blackhole	59
Molue	61
Colours Of Pain	63
Time's Triangle	70
Crane	72
Blackbird	74
The Pagan	76
Princess	79
Heaven Is Not Far	81
Bermuda Triangle: Angst Of The Past	83
Mari (For Mar Marburg)	87
Wings	89

III   Esoteric Voyage

Sacred paths	93
The Voyage	95
The Titans Are Coming	98
Night	100
In Search of An Extraordinary Man	102
Inner Voice	104
Cage For A Sage	107
Queen Of The Sphere	109
The Silent Voice	111
Time Traveler	113
Symphony Of Love	115

Landscape Of The Faithful · 117

IV   Political Musings

Trump Of Freedom · 123
This Farmland · 125
Pen of Wise Pigs · 128
A Spider's Web · 130
Songs Of Flood · 133

V   Love Chords

Homecoming · 137
Love Field · 140
Come To Me · 142
Your Fragrance · 144
Soulmate · 146
Oh, Little Faery! · 149
Uregwu · 151
Wings Of The Mind · 153
Desire · 155
Silhouette · 158
Bomadi · 160
Flower Of My Dream · 163
About the Author · 165
Also by Edentu D. Oroso · 167

Acknowledgement

I wish to acknowledge with profound thanks the invaluable contributions of friends, family members, and fellow poets whose support, advice, critique and encouragement helped to shape the content of this book into what it is today. My heartfelt appreciation goes to:

Ebiere, who tolerated me and held the forte through trying moments. Thanks for your love and care!

Stephanie, Preye, Angel, Tarebi, and Princess for making me smile even in the face of all odds! I love you all and always will!

Mar Marburg (Gypsy Mar), for being an exceptional friend! I thank God he brought you my way!

Subrato Deb, for a wonderful book cover design!

Members of the **Writers' League Benue State University Makurdi,** and the **Association of Nigerian Authors (ANA) Benue State Chapter,** for the positive feedback through peer-review.

Camellia Morris, for being an exceptional friend, sister and publisher! May God continue to bless and protect you richly!

Praise For Richer Than Pride

*'Oh woman, you pillar the sum of man's strength
Without your compass he is but a lost navigator.'*

From moving portraits of women to celebrating nature and the wonders of celestial visions on a cosmic scale, Edentu Oroso's poems all are but glowing of hope, if not aching for it. One cannot but be impressed by the multitude of his ideas and images, weaved in a delicate, sensuous yet deeply inspiring language.

All here is a 'wanton waltz of hearts', a 'swirl of world' beguiling us, assailing us, and finally conquering us with a profound and radiant lyricism which is more than bewitching and enthralling, but uplifting. Eerie, dazzling, beautiful poetry.

*'In our hearts there's a song,
The song is love and love is life.'*

-Aurélien Thomas, author of 'A Vow – A Collection of Love Poems'
(coming out soon)

"Edentu Oroso has written an eclectic book of poetry celebrating the strength and versatility of women, through the use of different styles and subjects. His style and diction are readable and clear. A book worth checking out, poems for all tastes to enjoy."

- Samantha Beardon, author of Caught in Passion.

I

Womanhood

Mother

Remove the faint shawls of decades.
   Remould the scattered glimpses of childhood –
   Loom forth, mother, from the thick fog of time
   As nature's most magnificent gift.

Take away your fervid glow from the tunnel,
   Pour not affection's balming water
   That insulates a long and perilous rift
   Mother, and life remains but an eternal blight.

When your sonorous lullaby tinkles the wind no more
   And the sweet chirps of twittering birds turn forlorn,
   Mother, the restless bundle on your wise laps you wean,
   Wistfully challenging my pain as mortal treachery.

When the storm and the stars come and cease
   A gift of rainbow rears in the horizon,
   Scurrying, you harness your broken dreams
   For you reckon, mother, with the hue of the future.

There's a lone light in the void of your being
   Kindling hope where it was once lost,
   The only clime you perceive in the fields of uncertainty
   To climb and cherish forever; and that joy you say is me!

Culled from Sentinel Online 2013 edited by Unoma Azuah.

Richer Than Pride (An Ode To Womanhood)

Bathe yourself no more in tears of anguish and despair
   Oh woman, you pillar the sum of man's strength
   On the rough ledge of human action;
   To you he comes for a soothing balm

When life's currents are swift and his mind riled;
   Your warmth gives him hope for a better tomorrow,
   Without your compass he is but a lost navigator;

But if he won't give you your right of place
   Even when you are the energy that feeds his ego,
   Just remember woman, it is out of foolish pride;

On the crest of the next tide you must ride fast
   And take back the strength that belongs to you.
   Whatever the circumstance, you are richer than pride

Culled from Sentinel Online 2013 edited by Unoma Azuah

Joy Is A Vaulted Song

Hang me not in the gallows, my folks
  Much talk about marrying many wives…
  How nice to be singly web, my folks?
  Do not think I have nine lives;
  For my sorrows I readily multiply,
  When I take more wives like you.
  The cloak of culture I would rather simplify,
  So I do not end up like you.

Joy is a vaulted song,
  A song seldom rendered by many mortals…
  Theirs is a discordant gong,
  Full of the rhythms of strife like spent flower petals;
  For joy is a stranger in polygamy's hood,
  Dark and grotesque in its entire cocoon;
  Do not ask of me to forever brood,
  Of the joy of life is tomorrow's boon.

Culled from the anthology Cerebral(ity) edited by Maria Ajima & Sam Ogabidu.

Widowhood

in ugly shades of dark black robes
   she wails hunched at a corner of the bare floor,
   no sure way out of the stifling ropes
   strung easily through culture's dreary door.

she mustn't peer beyond the hue of brown drapes
   nor claim her lost beauty back so soon,
   'cause the mouth tastes of very sour grapes
   plucked by the swift wind of death at noon;

yet, the loud gongs of kinsmen must sound
   gourdful of varied brews to the toast
   proud culture woken to take its due pound.
   who cares if the woman goes to roast
   when there are many frontiers to poach?
   her luck if she doesn't end up like a trapped 'roach.

The Veil

Why does it seem so dear
  That I hide my face behind a veil?
  A condition to bear.
  But a mind you cannot tell.

Mine is a helpless submission,
  Behind the mask a yearning;
  No bars can halt the mind's mission,
  Far gone on the paths of discerning.

When I prowl down the crescent,
  My guilt is wrapped up in a shroud;
  When you think my portrait is so decent,
  It's a glimpse of another fraud.

The Girl Child

Long is the history of my precious nature,
  I'm the fertile soil of the unknown future
  Upon which humanity's seeds know nurture
  But swallowed up in maddening torture
  My lot hinged on household chores;
  Would I ever know of other tinged shores
  Of inspired talks, honed intellect and respect
  When the only rungs of honour I must inspect
  Are spread in the dirty rungs of relegation?
  Who says my brother is not enthroned a king
  When his credentials are the songs we all sing?
  Well, to the forest I go to fetch my logs of wood.
  Soon, he'll come to ask for food.
  Do I have a choice, when I am the girl child?

Corpse Of An Old Woman

She fetches water, she fetches wood.
   She hurries to get her children some food.

Their uniforms are dirty, their sandals are torn,
   To mend their soles she must sell some corn.

Rain is falling, the hut is leaking.
   A helping hand the woman is seeking.

Husband has fever, son has headache,
   She goes to doctor, no one to forsake.

She makes a ridge, she makes a heap,
   Her children are scattered like lost sheep.

Her limbs are weak, her body hot,
   None remembers her medicine pot.

The woman is dying, villagers are wailing.
   Neighbours never knew of her long ailing.

Children are gone, husband is dead.
   Where would the old she lay her head?

Here comes her corpse, so pale and forlorn.
   None salutes her even with a simple horn.

Her corpse is tossed up and down.
   Nowhere to bury in the early dawn.

Not in our quarters, tradition forbids.
   That is the story on her in-laws' lips.

And so she exits unsung,
   Like a mound of cow dung.

II

Rhythms Of Life

Life

Let the damp clay know form
  in the condensation of light;
  far down the rung of radiation
  express the storm of animation.

Life; the song rustling through creation,
  rhythm of a once great void;
  your symphony is of an orchestration
  beyond mortal's mind;

And your enchanting dance we find
  in the mould of every atom rage;
  but up the spiral of consciousness
  your descent, and return gaze.

Let the playhouse be
  in the facsimile of the soul to see
  far below, the tale of the journey up;
  vortex of the shining spark.

Life; the pulse of every wind,
  bloom of heavenly seed;
  your cloak encapsulates human frailty
  and invigorates the thrust of its kind.

In the reel of reality,
  your origin ignites a search;
  a clamber to the mountain reach
  then a detour to the deepest deep.

Let the heart speak
  unchangeable language of aeons;
  firm the rim on the wheel of the clay,

expedite ascent over the next twist.

Life; the twang of a timeless guitar,
   a chime not of man-made toy;
   your silent flute echoes from yonder
   reaching human ears in awakening joy.

The arduous journey of your mystery begins
   through daunting hills and pleasant valleys,
   ascribing purpose to an already defined course
   of your speck within.

Butterfly

BUTTERFLY

Roll on, glide:
  Let wind beguile
  The horde's bride.
  Set sail the wile,
  Find the nearest harbour.
  Hopes flutter;
  Winged need labour,
  But your bread needs butter.

Voice Of The Earth

VOICE OF THE EARTH

Hear the lyre of time, listen to the whispering wind
    Feel the pulse of nature, see the great dance of the waves
    Touch the proud veins of the earth, touch the womb of ages
    Sound the depth of the sun, awaken the soul of life
    In joyous songs of birds, hear the messengers of time
    And through the spectre of life the voice of the earth:

Feel the pulsations of the rivers, dance to the drums of the seas
    Hear the silent flutes of aeons, signatures of the currents find
    Embrace the arms of the forest, relish in her timeless cuddle
    Fetch the jeweled leaves onto the shores of the now
    Bathe in the showers of ethers, speak the language of the spheres
    And in the light of the self the voice of the earth:

Marvel at the peaks of the hills, and the bowels of the mountains
    See the beauty of the ants, envy the harmony in their hills
    Drink the nectar of flowers, the sweet wine of the bees
    Praise the lilies of the valleys, sing the tunes of the trees
    Yield to the call of the stars, sway to the caress of the moon
    Above all, listen to the voice of the earth.

    Culled from the anthology Voice of the Earth *edited by Edentu D. Oroso & Sam Ogabidu*

Phoenix

PHOENIX

Men are not the sterner stuff of tales
   Unless like the Phoenix they stir corn-fields
   With their rise from the ashes of time,
   And like dough swell with the yeast.

Men are not always eagles in the sky
   That caper with grace and elegance
   In accord with the dictates of thermal currents,
   Unless they are weaned in the art of flight.

Men are but the relics of fertile imaginations
   That plods and prods through crackling corn-fields
   Brimful of great noise and grave silence,
   Unless they rise to the plaintiff cries
   Of plumeless birds in parched fields.

And regal are the stead of men when
   Their cycles of quest are gentle,
   No less rustled by humility's own spirit
   Taken to the bounds beyond the self;
   Then only is the proud Phoenix risen.

Culled from the anthology Voice of Earth edited by Edentu D. Oroso & Sam Ogabidu.

Water Dialogue

WATER DIALOGUE

Water: Listen, my ponds no longer ripple;
   your intelligent ignorance so scorches me dry,
   long winding streams find no beginnings
   from which to course through great plains;
   is this sign that mortals no longer find
   in their blood the stream of relevance?

Man: No action is ever still, noble companion,
   time re-orders everything, even your relevance;
   we've long passed where we were yesterday,
   we are far from where we hope to be tomorrow;
   but you are caught in the bug of advancement:
   the only hope is not to stand still.

Water: When the dumb feign to speak
   and the blind paint the colours of light,
   the keel is set for a plunge of no return;
   but upon which river would it glide
   when the flood carries murk eddies
   so strewn through the banks of advancement?

Man: Birds certainly will find their nests
   even in the darkest hours of night;
   upstream or downstream, we'll find our shores
   and row our canoes towards our ends.

Water: Oh, that heady song of swans:
   "Deep in the pool, but quench thirst upland!"
   I was part of our beginning,
   I know what remnant of you I'll wash
   even if you consider me an expendable fool.

Iroko

IROKO

And the anda ozi calls from the corner of the arena
    A beat so familiar that lifts up your spirit
    And memories of past calls swell your head
    Your proud veins come alive, and surge forth with dare
    Once more, the Iroko is called to a display of strength
    Yes, the gentle Cat is unleashed to skill

And with a blanket gird around your torso
    A jangling bell on your waist that echoes messages
    And the ogele of cheering cries of loved ones
    The Cat is transformed into an awesome Iroko
    Yet the Iroko must dance the dance of a Cat
    In fierce drama of skill and muscle

And the anda ozi calls loudly, forcefully
    The ogele becomes a frenzied lot
    As Iroko gyrates into the arena in defence of Okoloba
    Cries of confidence pelts the other from Torugbene
    The umpire's shrill whistle signals the tourney
    And the Cat must outwit the Rabbit in prance

Hands clash, feet thrash, eyes and muscles bulge
    The earth swoons beneath the forms in wedlock
    A raised leg, a twisted hand, an attempted throw
    The Iroko wriggles free, charges sideways, claps an ankle
    A tide of nerves to the rescue
    And the Rabbit groans with back on the bare earth

The Iroko who stood toe to toe with Ariri in the arena
    The Cat who bedazzled Emontongha to a deuce
    The throb of the arena, the pride of Okoloba
    Like sunlight in the dark plains of a tribe
    Like a lion bestriding the veldts of conquest

The Iroko dances around, smiles to the rousing cheers

- *Anda ozi: Big drum used during wrestling tournaments.*
- *Ogele: A procession of dancers cheering contestants at wrestling tournaments.*
- *Ariri and Emontogha: Names of prominent Izon wrestlers in the 1950s.*
- *Okoloba: An Izon town in Delta State, Nigeria.*
- *Torugbene: An Izon town in Bayelsa State, Nigeria.*

Circumstance

Some tides of life often toss us
   into borders of confusion; our minds
   court the crest of many turbulent waves
   and yield to downstream currents
   never given to strokes that lead upstream

…That's just circumstance, the pulse of another passing day

Some paths are denied the gift of light,
   such little weights of thought that hold us down
   and rob our minds of illumination;
   in the maze, we fumble and groin
   till we decide to act out our own script

…That's the mould of circumstance rearing on life's way

At times we swim against currents so swift,
   our minds' weights thrust upon our heads
   thinking it would descend and crush us to nothingness,
   where our voices retain no distinct echo
   and we live on like unwanted drafts in life's sea

…That's surely circumstance's silk, which we must not weave

When life deals us a gnarled hand
   our sky is a blanket of darkness; our sun
   recedes into the crevices of fearful thoughts;
   the flight of time ensnares hope,
   in the plains of denial, an incensed play

…That's just the weight of circumstance, the thing to shed

Morning Dew

The mountain is awash with morning dew...

Cindered earth pregnant with its rivulets,
   The flowering of the fields, signals of its essence;

The dew, great dew from the mountain top

Rolls away the catacombs of the sphere!

And the colony of ants rejoice over the choice
   The thrilling magic of its floodgates

Feel
   The cooling of the temperate climes

Song Of A Butterfly

Upon this lush savannah, I caper
And sing the melodies of sisterhood.

Across the valley, a vista of sun-burned lilies;
As I lift high over the green tapestry,
They beckon for the tenderest touch
To turn the valley's blight into a theatre –
For the gorged eyes of the savannah to feed on
As fractured hearts crave a new song.

So I hum a tune, as I caper;
I'll rock you to sleep with my enchanting colours,
And I'll sing for you the song of a butterfly
So that you too can someday fly,
Far and above the clutches of the savannah;
That's where you ought to be.

Culled from the anthology Cerebral(ity) edited by Maria Ajima & Sam Ogabidu.

Water

What alchemy in heaven's gate transformed you
   golden dust of the earth
   a thirst quenching medicine in river forms?

What portions in the dexterous hands of angels
   churned you, powerful blood of nature
   as the essence of all life forms?

Why, oh why, do all creatures owe you allegiance
   in the unfurling of their peculiar acts on this stage?

Why, oh why, do your wells in all cells when dry
   harbinger the very end of all creative quest?

They say you are a transmutation of elements –
   a legendary romance between hydrogen and oxygen
   when heaven's gate unleashed it creative vortex;

They say you are the cascading blood of the gods
   that seeks to balance intrinsic equation of nature;

They say there can be no marriage of convenience
   between the great silent forces without your consent;

We know there lies a nurturing bed in your greatness
   where the heavens and the earth meet in wedlock
   in the final assemblage plant of life and its forms.

Water; you're heaven's elixir through which we stir.

I Have Overcome

I've overcome the dark evil of night
  Cloaked in the primordial power of light;
  With the sharp scythe of the avenging Godhead
  Swung at the merchants of darkness
  Who feast upon my pains and beggarliness,
  I've overcome the dark hood of servitude
  Hung like a guillotine over my head;
  Alas, I'm free from the sorcery of evil's multitude.

I've overcome the power of primordial curses
  Invoked at the gates of the mountains of my graces
  For light knows no ransom
  Even in the tempest of vile courses,
  Like the Phoenix I arise once more wholesome;
  I've overcome ethereal powers of the air
  In the mystical aura of water I'm replenished
  By the energies of the earth I ascend;
  Alas, I'm a child of destiny.

Wisdom Lane

Child: On this narrow lane, I trudge daily
   What lesson there is to learn
   And how I fare, I don't know truly;
   Am I just another flowering fern
   Waiting to be discovered in the forest of being
   Or am I from reality fleeing?

Sage: Hardly a lane that remains undefined;
   Every flower opens up its petals to the sun
   And find the centre where its being is steeped;
   For every breath, there is a duty done
   But the lessons of this lane only unfold
   To the initiate whose self-story is told.

Fierce Sickle

Never a primer on swaying stalks
   that enact pristine orgies of creation
   upon arable plains
   The sickle's subtle swing
   burrows deep down life's enclave
   a spell of external hue cast
   on the chivalry of cell
   all in the zest of a fierce harvester

Never a hapless harvester of grain
   nor of the tuberous fibres
   that swell and swirl the earth's womb
   Not the stout sickle
   that makes the vibrant stalks cringe and yield
   to the caress of the harvester's whim
   This is the macabre harbor
   of a cell's mortal journey

The Edge Of Silence

Have you ever been there?
   The edge of silence.

Ever taken that lonely walk
   towards the precipice and seen
   the steepness of its yawning centre?

Have you ever seen the calmness
   of a storm that never whirs
   with the meaninglessness of sound
   at the steep edge of silence?

Have you ever been drawn
   like a cart on a mule's mirthless rein
   towards a storm's epicenter
   that's as calm as a stagnant pond
   and felt safe at the awful silence
   to which the heart's offerings are subsumed?

Have you ever taken that dive?
   Into the yawning warp of silence.

The silence of a thousand utterances:
   bubbled up in time's own heady currents
   of spent and jaded glimpses and memories
   of distant and barren canvasses.

Culled from the anthology Voice of the Earth *edited by Edentu D. Oroso & Sam Ogabidu.*
   Also published in Sentinel Online 2013 *edited by Unoma Azuah.*

Celestial Saucer

Clam-like saucer whirs down the void,
  Quaint hump like a shimmering dome,
  Ethereal dynamics ruffling swirling atoms,
  Bi-valve mass swift through celestial currents.
  Wheeled tripods cringe out
  As celestial saucer skirts earth.
  Radar zooms out like a hunting crane,
  And a not too distant neighbour pries.
  Horns reflect the nadir of intelligence,
  Her vast panels record baseness.
  In the timelessness of her aeon,
  She drifts into the sea of photons.

Once Upon A River Benue

The canoe glides against the river current,
   Her bow prodding gracefully through the expanse
   The wake of the front paddle caresses her sides,
   Next to the swelled banks of the River Benue;
   From her yawning bowel mother and child paddled
   Engaged in a merry muffled chatter,
   As the thick marches of the river speed bye.
   The flooded forest of huge trees
   Across the guileless river loom.
   Islands of drafts criss-cross her muddy surface
   Its full strength the canoe veers to test,
   Watched by the peaks of the Gbajimba hills,
   Tree-lined gates of the dreary forest
   Opened to the cock-a-doo chants of welcoming birds.

Just few moments of light before dusk,
   The canoe hobnob past immersed brushes
   And a dove-tail through swimming sturdy tree-trunks,
   Under the canopy of overhanging branches;
   Space to cast a net is sought
   In the tangle of water swept surfacing grasses,
   A raucous noise the child makes,
   "Shsssh!" the mother cautions. "Silence.
   Else we'll lose our net to lurking thieves!"
   An ear to the rustling leaves, the child listens!
   An owl hoots eerily, a school of monkeys stir,
   'Mama, are those eavesdropping thieves?" the boy asks,
   His mother chuckles; "Monkeys and pranks!"
   Net is cast as the sun goes deep down.

Culled from Bridge for Birds an anthology of poetry on Benue State, Nigeria edited by Sam Ogabidu and Sam Agwa.

The Rain

Splattering rain like some scud missiles falls
   Once more from the vaults of the heavens;
   Its staccato drums and leaps on the dry land
   Transformer of a farmer's sour mood.

He gyrates in salute of this benevolence,
   Chants in praise of the gods' fertility;
   Their seeds soon will sprout; rain's impregnation
   In the womb of mother earth.

The sun like some oven pours down its heat
   Denies the happy land again of fertility;
   He sighs and broods and prays for another splash
   A leeway for his unscathed tomorrow.

His visions' reins anchors on the land
   Pulled onwards by its good yields;
   When the kiss of the rain stops the cart of gods
   He's grounded for lack of positive initiative.

Poverty

It comes like a silent breeze,
   Gentle in its initial mission, intent
   Undisclosed in the increasing wheeze,
   Suddenly its tease becomes a painful patent.
   Its gale whips across a smiling face
   Renders a numbing slap,
   Stunning the mind with its fierce trace
   Revealing a hidden clap-trap,
   From which man attempts to escape;
   The demand of the forces' ransom, till
   He understands the nature of the landscape
   Leaves him prostrate and confused still,
   On the plain of worthless living
   Where his cries know no celestial resonance,
   Kindled by the moment's unpredictable phases, believing
   It won't forever be this strange hollow consonance.

Blackhole

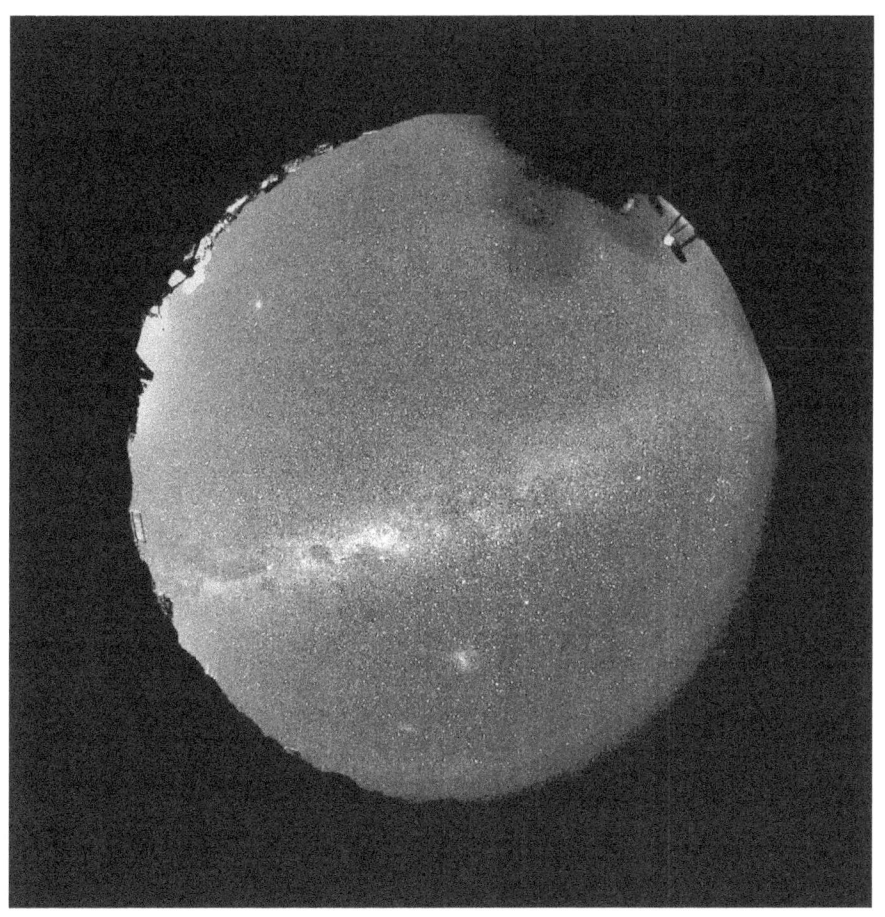

Look at the other realm
   Where the sun shines but scorches not,
   There's a Blackhole in the sun's beam.
   Gaze at the Blackhole's lot,
   See a Disc that glows and thrills.
   In the belly of the Disc,
   Sprawls infinite vortex frills,
   Where actions of creation are brisk,
   Defining aeons of time and space
   And of the tint of life,
   A form that reckons with no race.
   In life's womb all is life.

Molue

There goes madness, rickety molue:
  Jostle in and jostle out,
  Refuse to jump in and you're left out.
  Here comes the conductor, inflating madness:
  Push you here and push you there,
  The griot that knows everywhere.
  And the beat goes on.
  Hold the crossbar, stand apar;
  Buttocks to buttocks, the journey so far.
  Then comes the king of the molue:
  He shoves you, bumps into you,
  He's an expert at picking pocket too.

Colours Of Pain

imperial the rising sun
   great crimson disc in the distance
   in no hurry to make any tiring run
   over scurrying clouds in feeble resistance
   in the usher of dawn.
   even without tangible hearth
   the glowing flame encapsulates the earth;
   atoms twirl, molecules reshape randomly,
   a smouldering furnace of ideas,
   human aspirations are born
   all in the brilliant streak of morn!
   merry insects hop proudly on hosting grass
   twittering birds sing to the warmth of a new day
   jungles stir with the roar of rising beasts
   drowning their conquests, man's cymbals of brass
   under the agya of sunshine he scampers to make hay.

hopes rise and flare
   in the cast of Mount Everest,
   wanton tides that seem so rare
   beauteously cascading toward ego's crest
   assured of an anchor like imperial sun;
   but this is not the usher of another dawn
   when risen sun is permitted to fawn
   the invincibility of its sacred throne
   for hope's tide knows an incensing ebb,
   and morn's vortex of inspiration
   is the sire of the colours of pain:
   varied hues – harsh, sublime, hazy, cool
   that wouldn't take even the mind of a fool
   to discern the hidden lines of strain
   behind the radiance of mortals' quests.

even a great smile may be from the vault of pain
  just as the sun knows the hurt of defiant cloud
  that must roll away over the horizon like vagrant train.
  pain's badge avails an unwelcome immunity
  spreading its weight like a damn shroud
  which deadens every instinct to cry aloud;
  and who will listen to a pauper's whimper
  under the steamroller of the privileged puppeteer?
  he is but another lost mariner
  whose zeal is silenced in the oceans of time;
  in frenetic search for his broken compass
  he hopes for a sweet ride on the next tide
  to give his wobbling ship the windward sail
  that would haul him to the first pageant island;
  and at the hazel harbour of this pleasant land
  a helping hand – and no colours of pain.

each dawn renews his vigour and hope
  defying the perilous fringes of despair
  he leans tenuously on fate's inexplicable rope,
  the hollows of empty dreams he fills
  with a cache of broken promises;
  butt of everyone's naked lies: the state, colleagues and family
  yet he reckons with their intervention as timely
  as if his wreck they will soon repair
  and send his ship sailing down gold streams.
  in spite of their raucous and insistent rally
  he's caught in the thick web of callous society;
  a taunt of defiant and poisonous flies
  explains leering grimaces and overt cackles
  from those that once patronized him with their banal lies;
  and they say pain was long extinct from earth terrains,
  if it exists, it's the colour of the king that rules his mind.

the air rents with a child shrill whining,
  his listless and fangled form his mother cuddles
  and feels the stab of hunger from the jagged rib bones;
  into rheumy eyes, pale brown and sunken, she peers
  the shadow of a ghost stares back at her,
  squirming in fear, tears squirt her own eyes;
  there's no grain in the barn –
  merciless blight consumed the young farm
  pallid breasts she thrusts into parched lips
  stifling the child's whining with a discordant yarn;
  child nibbles and recoils from the feel of flaccid teats
  once full wells of milk now dry as a barren desert;
  coins expended on the tasteless gruel of yesterday,
  ten kilometers walk on a rickety road to nearest clinic
  neighbours couldn't offer even a modicum of hope;
  they too had seen the strange colours of pain.

she swings her haunches through the clinic's gate,
  pale form of son speaking volumes of death's date;
  doctor reels out a gurney, runs for his stethoscope
  theatre's door slams shut, hands and machine hobnob
  in frantic haste to save the dying child;
  there's light out, machine grins to a halt
  anesthetics fail, hands quiver, nerves wrack,
  forlorn mumble from behind the theatre's door;
  nurses race towards the pharmacy
  they return with no drugs in tow;
  the brush of pain now etched on their grim faces
  stroking its way into their guarded emotions;
  no drugs to feed the veins of the child they inform her
  the woman wails; fate why are you so cruel?
  doctor's crestfallen – offers blind words of courage,

but even in his eyes gleaned the colours of pain.

school bells toll along gaudy streets,
   sparks of ambition fly through a boy's head
   like ambient crackle of restoked fire;
   he wheels homeward to his mother's treat
   lunch park in hand and books to read,
   hurries toward school with a burning desire
   to climb someday the peak of the Ivory Tower
   and feel the glory that the peak will shower
   for the wonder and worth of his young life he was told
   lies in the uncanny paper of an endorsed paper
   without which he is just as good as sold
   not even worth the price of a cheap wrapper
   on the racks of the labour market;
   aims his dart in school at a unique target
   assiduously working towards the climax
   unaware of the colours of pain that haunt his stead.

under the sun's scorch and heavy splatter of rain
   parents' toil to lay the carpet of his fragile future
   colours of pain unmasked in their austere meals
   and the stacks of time worn clothes they adorn
   denying selves life's pleasures to brighten his day;
   he vows to give them back their lost world
   after crossing ambition's own rubicon –
   on their gaunt faces will rear bright smiles,
   exotic meals will grace their dining table
   and life will seethe with a new rupture;
   a child from another time and race he must be,
   here's not the right place for utopian visionaries;
   the bleakest of landscapes his inheritance on graduation
   hope dead; future fanged in the horrid colours of pain,

cordoned in a vicious cycle from which there's no escape.

yet at the centre of a high sounding fora,
   mannequin on display, grinning like silly sheep –
   country man walks up the scarlet podium
   talks with the sleek tongue of a rogue,
   with nice clichés and oratory power
   engages the masses in another mind game;
   the young man is stunned by the polemics of power,
   though con artist's milk flowed from the people's pain,
   naïve horde surge forward in eager bid to taste of his opium,
   he couldn't blame them, it's their only password to stardom;
   no succour even in the wig from the Ivory Tower,
   none gives a hoot if he'd waltzed between the walls of school
   until hunger fangs shoves him to scrounge from garbage cans
   man on the podium sees no colour of pain in the gnash of teeth;
   but why did the boy's forebears flaunt the Ivory Tower
   if at the end he's no better than peers living off squalid streets?

an itchy hand snaps a trigger,
   the bang of a gun in the thicket of a gaudy alley
   a scream or two, a body staggers in rude spasms and falls;
   another round of rallying salvos – more bodies writhe,
   it isn't hard to tell the ugly nature of the parley
   from the awe-struck mob around hideous stalls,
   it's a pageant of hoodlums;
   their appetite for the fast life whetted by the dapper stranger
   with the gold rings, wristwatch and exquisite briefcase;
   a mother mourns, wife and kids curse fate
   but the hoodlums only see it as silent war
   against the womb that brought forth their misfits,
   they too are mascots in the lingering vortex of pain;
   if the man on the podium is inviolate

then he'd better consider his next of kin as late
it's the only recompense for the colours of their pain.

on the chessboard of chance
  the one who understands the gambits
  schemes his way to the glitzy heights,
  while those who languidly wait for a pious prance
  somewhere beyond the corners of earthly orbits
  are relegated to the backdrop by circumstance –
  both are ensnared in existential ironies;
  at the heights, there's a realization –
  too many lies weaved to make his station hold
  like heady flies he must carry on with his charade of deception,
  his smiles coated with the strange colours of pain;
  but how would the kingpins of the dark know
  that the man that fawns the silver spoon
  and the one who roasts in squalid cocoon
  are identical twins sharing varied colours of pain
  and differ only in the shades and strokes of pain's portrait?

Time's Triangle

TIME'S TRIANGLE

A soft wind whistles by at dawn
    teasing with a mystery we do not know…
    Splendid the wake of sunrise in the spawn
    a hint tinged in its crimson glow;
    So clear is time's own jingle
    of tomorrow's rhythms in the sky.
    And we wait to know its tinkle
    like a caterpillar into a butterfly.

A bird scurries to its nest
    shying away from the scorch of the sun…
    But its zeal must know the test
    entwined with the day's swift run;
    Back into the wild fields it goes
    resplendent in its airborne wings.
    Against the fierce storm's throes
    a display of its daring swings.

And ego is fed by an afterglow
    near the dreary fringes of sunset…
    A wish to escape this subtle blow
    yet nature has won its simple bet;
    Sunrise is long gone, day is somewhat spent,
    Curtains of dusk inspire a new reckoning.
    If only life was on the market stalls for rent
    it would hearken to our ardent beckoning

Crane

CRANE

The Crane swoops down the river bank,
   A white-washed mass on the river's mirror.
   Her spindly legs ripples the sluggish currents
   As beady eyes scan the shallow depths.
   Her mind keen on scurrying fish,

The Crane plunges her neck like a taut bow
   Deep into the currents a rummage for a meal,
   A thrashing fish in her honed beak,
   Respite comes in a strenuous swallow.

Her huge wings swoon again into the sky
   And a proud fisher squawks back to its nest,
   Where this harvest she regurgitates,
   The famished cries of her young are silenced,
   Back to the river bank an impassioned Crane.

Blackbird

BLACKBIRD

Every morning nature's primer comes across the meadow,
   This flamboyant but lithe Blackbird and perches so free
   On the overhanging branches of the nearby tree
   Like an automated contraption over my window,
   Just before the wake of dawn.

His sing-song in the chilled morning air, as ever
   By the priming of an unknown lever,
   Infringes on my soul's excursion into the abstract lawn;

"Wake up and pray! Wake up and pray!" his patented chirps,

And I stir awake with a faint grudge in my heart.

"Now, look inwards! Look inside of you!" his nudging start,

Languidly I hearken to these prompting chirps,
   And triumphant Blackbird vanishes into the mist of dawn.
   If these are daydreams at reality's fringes
   Which entrances the mind with delusive tinges,
   Not radiant Blackbird that would come not only at dawn.
   Proud harbinger of encrypted tidings,
   Stunts over the balcony once out of his unseen nest

Keen on his errand to keep me abreast,
   From the intangible comes his noon-song findings;
   "Mother is coming. She's coming home!" Blackbird's song.
   Ding-dong, the doorbell rings fifteen minutes later,
   And there stood mother grinning by the door, coming for a letter,
   Never has my primer Blackbird been wrong.

The Pagan

THE PAGAN

The grove appeared vibrant, libations quite
   Potent. The custodian propitiates the rites
   Of ancestry. Statutes of self-actualization
   Exulted.

"Look" he boasted cheerily,
   "A proud child of providence – nature's my mother."

Loud sneer. Sneering sounds from alien
   Spheres. Hues of doctrinaire culture,
   Tasteless gruel shoved easily down his
   Dry throat. His invaluable compass seemed lost.

"Ignorant Pagan"...cursed the visitor...
   "Would you like to know the way out of this fetish jungle?"

Flannel shirt. Flannel trouser.
   White bi-focal spectacles. Black polished shoes.
   Inflated portrait of many astounding lies. Scriptures unscrolled.
   Arrested, conscion on the mortgage – forcing surrender
   Of the custodian's basic intelligence. This is the deal! Graft of
   Estranged values in the gush of ill-transferred hatred.
   A determined visitor, drumming his point –

"With your grove you remain a pagan.
   Condemned! With the Scriptures you're one with the true GOD!"
   Reckoning time….

"A veritable old man on his throne in the sky – you mean?"

The visitor's anger palpable, hot wind of Derision laden in his breath.
   Hastily parallels are drawn. The Custodian assuaged.

"I know heaven and your true God"

Adding, *"Isn't it the experience of the light within?"* Shocked

Muteness, visitor's critical appraisal of the other's wisdom.
   Again the storm of wits.

"Don't blaspheme, Pagan!" insisting

"Libations are outmoded: Devoid of divine light."

"Like your scriptures' deceptions?"
   "The word confirms truth."

"Not exactly! Signpost of truth, but sir, absolutely...

Truth is a transcendent experience. Practical shuttle
   Into the ocean of consciousness. A pagan you brand me,
   But I possess that which you crave – creation's prized cipher.
   Pertinently sir – between your belief in recycled stories and my
   Practical inner-self gaze for guidance, *who is the real pagan?"*

"Nonsense! Absolute nonsense! Damn heretic!" fuming

Retreat of the visitor.

"I'm not done sir. Mind if I show you the Cenotaph of my soul?
   You see no divine light there too?"

Princess

No longer an obscure page in enduring fable,
   The awed heroin of a vaulted sphere,
   Weird heiress, goblin of your forsaken table,
   Your cold splendour underneath water's square –
   No longer there does the majestic PRINCESS stare –
   Dolling doom styxed commands of a professed rabble
   The innocent dawn is scathed: soon over her fare
   High-handed shall they maintain their sinister stable.

But no, not under cover of placid water, but here,
   In the terrains of the living, close to the cause of their ache,
   Vengeance stirs like a tornado thrashing here and there
   And man stumbles feebly stunned by the fierce take,
   Then scampers blindly in bid to escape to somewhere –
   Devoid of the clawing hands of PRINCESS.

Heaven Is Not Far

Heaven is not far,
   Not a long shuttle to a distant star
   But a recast of human thought.

Heaven is not far,
   When the pulse of every heart
   Knows no spite and suspicion from the start.

Heaven is not far,
   In the birth of fierce ambition
   A sure respect for human value.

Heaven is not far,
   When the eyes perceive no colour
   And race distinction is given no fervour.

Heaven is not far,
   Not the absence of drummed peace
   But the presence of intrinsic love.

Heaven is not far,
   From a heart devoid of greed,
   Where selflessness has painted a seed.

Heaven is not far,
   When nature's bounties are tinkered
   For the good of our humanity.

Bermuda Triangle: Angst Of The Past

Across the roiling haze of vast sea
   far, far away in the budding splendour of a continent
   profuse the discourse of men over cups of hot tea
   such morning waffling that seemed pertinent
   echoing with the pleasant chants of Eureka!
   as roving binoculars made bare, with no seeming replica
   the unspoiled treasures of mother Africa.

Spun on the wheels of spurious quest
   allure of her gold and boundless spirituality
   answered ambition's strange request
   and men set sail on the raft of perceptuality
   feigned towards the shores of the far cleft
   tossed to hone the other humanity long slept
   an embryo of civilisation they flaunt they long left;

Merry shore of Africa soon knew the sad drone
   of berthed alien ships and men of heady zeal
   a proud landmass shook as ego's fierce zone
   conscience was mortgaged in the new deal
   and a continent riled in her darkest moment
   partition and enslavement, a people's torment
   their profound values derided in the other's forment;

In the return journey to distant land
   exalting in the wind of swift conquest
   thrilled by the mystique of Africa's impeccable sand
   custodians of the divine crucible, the strangers' sudden request;
   hordes of transcendent peasants were the hauled cargoes
   in seaward alien ships, and there goes
   intrinsic wisdom of ages, hence, Africa's woes.

Mid-sea, the first strident chimes of dissent

piercing strange halos of ships' decks like struck chord
captives own defiance of precipitous descent
threatening smooth sail in psychic accord;
but the captors won't allow their ambition doused
deep in the extrasensory storm, new inspiration was aroused
fleece the gifts of knowledge – into sea custodians slouched.

From within filthy bowels of sailing ships
   fettered humans dragged out like worthless iron shaft
   under brutal guns they were a herd of scared sheep
   delving without a choice into secrets of the divine craft;
   then in the glare of hungry sharks and whales
   gloating captors cart the frightened human bales
   to see inevitable fate before the ships' rails;

And into the great triangular spawn
   between Bermuda's horn, Nassau and Florida
   went the last binge of the captive's drowning drawl
   emergent bent in the fine prong of the divine fork;
   survivors sailed in chains to harness the other splendour
   but the spirits of their blood brothers gained new ardour
   in the chasm of the Triangle, tasking humans in fierce clangour.

When the strange knell of vengeance begins to toll
   human memory acknowledges but its improbable mystery
   time tuned vortex of recycled energies in seabed roll,
   censored are the crafts of newly splendored history
   gains of the intellect denigrated in the charged spawn
   subsumed into the crypt of an abstract dawn,
   man's sure recompense for yesterday's pawn;

Bermuda Triangle, angst of Africa's past travails
   forlorn echoes of your blood brothers' arduous journey,

garnered palls of incensed authority now prevails
and the progenies of its weird cause are called to tourney;
but who would assuage the rage of the once silent gods
in sacred pantheons without their scepters and divining rods,
or potent libations splashed at sturdy roots of long felled logs?

Mari (For Mar Marburg)

Angels seldom caper to arid plains
   With wings flapping in soft wind
   Seeking out souls on the edge of the precipice
   Except in propitiation of pristine duties.

Angels rear and rave in our subconscious
   Not always in toga of aliens
   Courting a sense of awe and mystique
   With their cadences, power and beauty.

In many guises do Angels plod upon life's plains
   Their smiles and actions sets them apart
   from the motley crowd of mortals.
   Mari wears that hood; an Angel in disguise!

Wings

Give me wings

I'm a dawn awakening
   over night's hood

Not this assemblage of metals
   a pilgrim of the shores

Give me wings

With an eagle's strength
   to swiftly test the currents

III

Esoteric Voyage

Sacred paths

As your guest great furnace of life, I consider you fair
   Stranger to your embrace, your brimming fire welcomed me
   In the molten lava of experience, raw gold, baptized
   Poured forth in the melting, stretching, moulding
   Unto the morning dews on sacred paths
   And there I sparkle, a hard core brilliance

As host, refining fire of life, you consider me worthy
   Turning and twitching and turning on your grille
   Crossing the borders of the waves of your drill
   Sights fixed on no less a hue than the hallowed heights
   Now, a widening consciousness, and a new prize
   That's how you define my character of change

The Voyage

Rise, great Muse, from the great spheres;
  Show your hand in the craft of this art

Guide the soft sail of this tall tale
  Lest in mortal memory, I weave not the Muse's craft

Bid your bud the scented sprout of wisdom,
  As I weave time's threads in the voyage's loom.

Retrieve anchor, turn the ship windward,
  Marvel, the roiling rolling towers of water

Seven, the sunlight sprays, seven, the blue blanket nights;
  Of noise of silence, great voices of the Triangle

Let me, great Muse, the splice of time to tell;
  Of the vaults of creation so suddenly slit

Of primordial voice, echo from the core of photons
  To put to indelible ink the spirals of being

Of gardeners, architects, engineers, etched in transit plains
  The sphere's chest of ageless intelligence

Remind me, great Muse, the holy howling of wind
  Power horse of earth, in the banal romance with photons

And voice of aeons call in the depth of the wind;
  Go, child of the realm, harness the free flood of ethers

And the deep to my wandering mind calls
  Earth's frame, soul and spirit, banished in the Triangle

THE VOYAGE

Creation's till, chest of earth's enchantment
   Yet, its placid vastness so deceptive

Echoes from the deep, all of my pens drain
   Weaving the yarns of sacred secrets

So the permission, flood of vision, Triangle to leave
   And the crew awoke in the passing haze.

The future tilled, and in the voyage sprouts
   Sunshine ripened frits, for those who seek.

And earth forms remain brimful thereafter.

   Culled from Transcendence: Anthology on Human Thiought edited by ...

The Titans Are Coming

THE TITANS ARE COMING

When the day dims and the golden glimmer of an age
   Wears no more the hood of its proud beginnings,
   The gardeners will once more prune their fields:
   The Titans are ploughing!

When all else is noise, and the fury of the ascent
   Robs the light of day and enthrones dusk at dawn,
   The silver skies will once more split with meaning:
   The Titans are sowing!

When the stars starkly sing of their toil
   To keep us abreast of the sea to which we plunge,
   Know the big bell of time has tolled:
   The Titans are reaping!

When even breath is fouled by earth's own dust
   And the sun and the moon are no longer in concert
   And the earth cringes to its own resonance:
   The Titans are here.

Culled from the Sci-Fi/Fantasy Titan Race *by Edentu D. Oroso*

Night

NIGHT

night is the time of day
   day is the time of night
   voice is the sword of escape
   escape is forged in vigil

speak to the night it great language
   amid the prowl of night miscreants
   watch their constructs crumble
   in the rage of a fearless voice

night respects not the snores of slumber
   honours hearts on the watch
   night unfolds frontiers of battle
   where ethers clash in random motion
   finds in ego a willing undertaker
   in the seamless sail of reason

night is not the time of day
   when noise is silence
   silence is not the time of night
   when noise is might
   sound the drums of war, rouse the ethers
   seek the winds on which to fly
   into the splendour of your rest

In Search of An Extraordinary Man

I set out in search of an extraordinary man,
   Yet I found only an ordinary man
   Doing ordinary things in extraordinary ways;
   Neither a genie, nor a giant
   But conscious is he of his potential;
   Through the power of his creative imagination,
   Generates lofty visions, great hopes and desire.
   The impossible are the stuff of his visions,
   In the incredible lie his fervent beliefs
   So he achieves the extraordinary,
   And on the rungs of the super humans he's placed,
   An icon we admire and look up to.

I set out in search of the greatest warrior,
   Yet I found only the conqueror of self,
   A master of his thoughts, beliefs, and emotions;
   But craves harmony with self, and then with all things,
   Excellence being his due reward,
   His crafts are the building blocks of the mind;
   To win the battles of life he applies the will
   His memory must inspire his dreams and visions.
   Just as his emotions must positively rule his body,
   Truth is the healing balm of his conscience,
   And imagination casts his reality.

Inner Voice

INNER VOICE

Shut is the outside world.

A paling darkness the eyes see,
    And only a stuffed hum the ears hear
    In the inward grope to the other realm.

Then a brightening dawn.

The gift of an eye,
    There's a subtle lift from the shroud.
    A voice is restored,
    So tinged in celestial echoes.

That new form with the intrinsic gait
    Listens to the blissful harmony of self:

Rhythms of an unknown lyre.

To and fro the inner voice guides,
    Excited form drifts to view the sphere,
    And spies the trail of the damp shroud.

There's another radiant hedge;

A finer lift,
    The shuttle continues.

Form is no longer the shroud's captive,
    That redefinition of being,
    A contact with the source.

Then the dreariness of the shroud returns;

The voice is drowned,
   In the discordant echoes of living.

Cage For A Sage

Reveal truth and they persecute you,
  vilify you, mudsling you,
  Reveal knowledge and they hunt you,
  and a cage for a sage.

Join the bandwagon and they hail you,
  they adore you, revere you,
  Deceive them and they will ever flaunt you
  even in their wildest rage.

Awaken their sleeping souls and they turn on you,
  turn you, hate you,
  Rekindle their lives' light and they break you,
  not ones for self-realisation.

Take them beyond time and space, heretic they brand you,
  Reject you, alienate you,
  Talk only of the mundane and they will exalt you,
  in books, their gates to self-actualisation.

> *Culled from* Voice of the Earth *an anthology of poetry edited by Edentu D. Oroso and Sam Ogabidu.*

Queen Of The Sphere

The currents swirl in circles down the river
   Tossing the simmering reflection of the crescent moon.
   From beneath the bobbing mirror of this river,
   The rising twirl of a midnight sport soon:

An aura of great legends,
   Waist long curls of fleecy golden hair,
   Captivating beauty that sustains legends,
   Queen of the sphere rises to breathe fresh air.

Her sparkling scale and fin
   Subtly rippling the ever subservient currents,
   And her favour many seek to win
   In the hoopla of reliogo-mystical torrents.

She's come from her aqueous domain
   To stamp her awed authority on the mundane,
   A cauldron of evil so remain
   After a midnight orgy that's so insane.

Sprightly she swoons back to her sphere,
   Her decoys stashed everywhere,
   An endless chess of manipulative intelligence everywhere.

The Silent Voice

In the stillness of time and reason,
   Turbulent currents of the mind's raft
   Shore away in the crevices of alien clime,
   In sync with the toss of the inner raft
   Soul retrieves anchor and sets sail,
   Gently it glides towards the expanse of consciousness
   Calming the senses of earthly derail,
   Dawning reality of its ageless preciousness;
   Then the tingling moments of self-rebirth,
   As quietened mind finds due berth,
   At once the great echo of the silent voice
   In multiple streams of consciousness, the unmistaken choice,
   Of the ageless voice that consistently fulfill,
   All priceless visions and mortal aspirations re-till.

Time Traveler

I'm a time traveler
  On this craggy ledge of being
  Time and time again this contour I've seen
  In cloaks varied and true

Form is the ultimate weight to shed
  And experience is the compass that guides
  Through the twists and turns on the path
  Upon which growth is evidenced in the ascent or fall

I'm a time traveler
  Twirling down from the Light for the meaning of self
  Time and time again I've foraged through the dusky dawn
  To feel the intrinsic pulse of the magic of being

Entombed by circumstance in the matrix
  As a pilgrim, I must wrest off the stifling hands
  And find the upward paths of my beginnings
  For there lies my predestination

Symphony Of Love

A symphony of love
   Filters through the universe
   As the composer of man twangs his guitar.
   The song is life,
   An orchestration of love.
   Distant stars sing its glory,
   Its wonder neighbouring birds harp about,
   A rhythm the mountains rock to,
   We are all the pulsations of love.
   Love's harmonica serenades the river currents,
   The rhythm permeates the airwaves,
   In our hearts there's a song,
   The song is love and love is life.

Landscape Of The Faithful

Landscape of the faithful - - Ah, mystique of a near horizon!
The gaze, all the emotions, seems an enduring séance;
The proselytes plunged and stroked eagerly toward the far zone,
And no trials could wrest them off this unique trance:
Inspired in their stead, their visions' quality had a fragrance
Of life's radiant stuff they so pledge,
Like brilliant sunflowers awakening after night's hindrance,
Aglow with new exhilarating warmth, onto life's ledge
An outpouring from the celestial ceiling, they must acknowledge.

ii

Their long walk so virile, these ardent, pious elect,
They gave their selfless visions and lives in service to humanity,
And inwards their duty always to reflect,
Upon the vast landscape of being, shorn of profanity:
Their souls, on the other side, seems to soar to infinity,
Released from the dreary, weighty cloaks of form;
Sun-stars, moons, planets, interplay in light's inchoate profundity
And they soar by: growing in the soul's enchantment, as the norm
In order to transcend earth's fierce storm.

iii

No oars of time rippled in them desires long banished,
And scarce an effort, without the throbbing rhythms of devotion
Flavoured milk from peace's breast these elect were promised;
Their lives shimmered like sparkling stars in motion
Seeking to rid the land of its horde of hooded evil:
Another sheathed sword it seems is drawn, and soon the war
Declared in patches beyond in manner so civil,
And the horde of the dark kept vigil, wary of the sparkle from afar.

iv

That clash of opposites sounded notes of a prelude,

And the schemes unleashed, in the bowels of spawn so wide,
From dusk to dawn, shuttle of souls, each to elude
The glistening, roving blades that so seek evil's haughty bride:
A level playing field set for justice's ride,
And the Guardians of the realms umpire the contest:
The fugitive horde, ever guilty of blood cauldrons, hide
From the glare, where on return, the messengers find rest
With their halo restored, having won the earthly test.

v

From a safe distance, the retreating horde's loud protest,
With infernal rage, they defy the Guardians' rich array,
Plumes of defeat shed, renewed with thoughts of conquest;
The prelude is long gone, time for a new foray
When the arsenals of war turn in the other's way,
The bearers of the shield of the stars reassess their stand
Of the nights and days of sleepless saintly say,
On the tide of love that weaved them into a lofty band
That set forth as its own craft of heavenly brand.

IV

Political Musings

Trump Of Freedom

Arise, kindred souls, to eternal wakefulness
   For the silver skies hold the trump of freedom
   A banner once wrenched from the world
   By the monstrous hands of man's selfsame ogre

Arise, slumbering spirits, see the freedom skies
   Unlikely apparitions in strange firmament
   No more to disappear forever, and ever
   For it's the prize of our eternal vigilance

Come hear its flutes in every sound
   And hear its howling force in everything
   Never had it departed our great shores
   Only imagination allowed torment of our condition

Now you must see nothing without seeing it
   Now you must hear nothing without hearing it
   And you must feel nothing without feeling it
   For it gazes down on you from every shining star

In every calm sea lies its smile
   In the gush of every wind you'll hear its breath
   And it's the poetic motion in every storm
   It is the trump of freedom

This Farmland

This sprawling farmland –

like strokes etched deep in the womb of the sun
   uniquely spread over the boulders of the moon
   watched by the tender arms of the stars:

Did you not marvel at its expanse and beauty
   with enlivened thoughts about its fecundity?

This verdant farmland –

of rustling corn-fields and swaying rice stalks
   and the ever brilliant tint of pregnant tubers
   bulging forth from the livid veins of the earth:

Were we not blest to be so hosted in paradise
   with its cache of bounties and experience?

This great farmland –

tinged with long history of hydrocarbons
   stacked in the bowels beneath corn and rice fields
   and in the deep cauldrons of the Atlantic:
   Did we not chant 'hosanna' to the barrels
   of the earth's blood that fed our naked desires?

But this quaking farmland –

that sends birds and rodents scampering afield
   into their nets and burrows
   for fear of thunder's clap
   and the torrent of wasteful rain:

THIS FARMLAND

Would our corn-fields still sway with zest and life?

And this endless lightning –

that so blind the harvesters from sowing
   the seeds for tomorrow's great seed
    that makes them sink under the weight of harvest:

Is that the lot of this farmland?

Culled from the anthology In the Crosshairs, *selected poetry by Ayo Gutierrez.*

Pen of Wise Pigs

Graft's but an art when the craft
   is mastered in the putrid pen of wise pigs;
   Graft's but graft when fevered fools
   indulge themselves after the ways of pigs' pen.

The pig that wields the might is but king
   in the jungle of beastly canter;
   The fool that imagines self as pageant pig
   reckons not with the unfair banter of life's camels.

   Culled from the anthology In the Crosshairs, *selected poetry by Ayo Gutierrez*

A Spider's Web

A SPIDER'S WEB

He lacks the roar of a lion,
   But my spider knows his onion
   Up above the swirling jungle,
   A loom of moistened yarn to the juggle;

Just like the pack of leopards and lions rumble
   Down below the great gassy tumble,
   His climb up the tree unhastened,
   By some inspiration his eyes glistened;

In patient strides his silky thread spins
   Safe where no ally or foe leans;
   Nestled in this web of fine gossamer,
   More lethal than sledge hammer.

Ambition soon fetches its food
   In the ritual of beasthood.
   The jungle quakes from cacophonous roar,
   The spider contrives instant oar;

Rows her ship out of turbulent water,
   Rapt like an expert rafter.

On the web's path the keel's sail,
   Hungry and angry beasts all hail
   Figured glide towards spider's nest,
   Where their resilience is put to test.

The keel floats into the yawning web;
   Ingenious spider knows it's never an ebb,
   The gaze beyond still has its tide
   Just the kind of code to make them abide.

End of the lions and leopards' roar has come,
   All must tend to the spider's become.
   Not in the character of beasthood,
   Those eloquent dialogues of priesthood;

Now's the time for double speak,
   As spider's zeal silences the strong and weak.
   And the marathon match of wits so rings,
   None is sure what portends it brings;

And there goes the dribbler on the turf,
   Kindled by the language of the tough.
   Between the scripted players he rolls the ball,
   Stalling for time to flaunt his gall.

And the jungle's peace murdered forever,
   No more display of the lion's mien, ever
   As spider spins and spins his yarn.
   Hungry elephant got denied in his barn;

And the agonies of the elephant echo through the land
   Spider is safe in his net, loot in hand.

Songs Of Flood

We may once more hear the howling songs; these cascades
   from Lagdo that cuddle vast frontiers of river basins.
   Angst from primordial currents from up-flung river…
   we may once more hear the howling songs; these cascades.

Tango of stout over-stuffed walls and bustling waters
   ruffling new depths, with new scale of effluents
   that wrest the grains of toil and creativity's gems
   which the Kingfisher curries in pitched crooning.

Stolen swathes of earth and edifices so subdued
   like Poseidon's hefty dose of tide on drifting Odysseus ;
   We may once more hear the eerie drone of scurrying beasts,
   this strange excursion of arrant fish in splendored homes.
   Fate's twist! I, proud Tilapia from far-flung depths,
   waltz now upon gilded thresholds and peer
   through tints of human secrets, the tapestry of life;
   For Lagdo's offerings, I'm now the Manor's heady king.

But neither Kingfisher nor I can boast of eternal toasts,
   these currents that we crest are no more than frills
   of blind bats that are yet to reckon with their folly
   in the natural priming of things of which we discern .

great spectres may once more elude the spawn!
   unless bridges find placement between gorged hearts
   or the safety of earlier depths I once more feel,
   and the Kingfisher to the warmth of his nest return.

V

Love Chords

Homecoming

i
   now the pulses flutter
   in the great convergence
   beyond the veldts;
   a peacock's homeward bound.

soon proud heart will cede
   the last feathery flight,
   and the fervent kiss sealed.

hips and hands and lips
   trump magical rhythms
   in the wanton waltz of hearts.

ii
   let the earth swoon
   beneath your form
   by our prompt libations
   under the glare of crescent moon.

and the bards hum their tunes
   in time's big belly
   bonding our essence,
   beyond the reach of mere mortals;
   the tune of homecoming
   of Uregwu the firefly.

iii
   then it's your turn to strike
   the strings of our sweet lyre.

now the ripened fruits:

pregnant moon extends a hand –
and a smiling Siamese in the sun.

Love Field

LOVE FIELD

There goes the queen of myriad dreams
   And her dainty walk so thrills, it seems
   The enchanting rhythm of a great song,
   Just the kind that makes the heart know no wrong;
   Her flight over the sphere's like a faery's
   And swift my search for gilded berries,
   By some stunt of instinct she shies away
   But there again she would come another day,
   Melting my resolve with her glorious smiles.
   My queen beautiful, and full of wiles,
   Kindled against the splendor of my dreams,
   And there she listens to the song in the wind
   Whistling across this love field of a kind.

Come To Me

COME TO ME

Sing to me with the voice of a Nightingale;
   Sing with the moving magic of your gait;
   Sing of the pulse of the wandering wind.

As fingers on guitar's strings,
   Strike me the chords
   My Nightingale, dance, come away from the pastures.

This song how nice, too nice, too loud
   Whose band wakes the cringing soul
   Where the pastures meets the glitz;

When the pregnant calabash sways
   To the pride of your heart
   In the mix of sorghum spice.
   Yet you sing to me in voice so real
   Turning my inner strings into a sweet harp;

So come sing to me of the heart's seal
   Thought for thought, rhythm for rhythm
   Come away, break away
   As glitz calls, my Nightingale, how glitz calls.

Your Fragrance

YOUR FRAGRANCE

You act like a rose;
   And your fragrance is a ruse
   Like craft of a Muse.

Soulmate

SOULMATE

on life's wondrous ship
  we sail forth as soul
  through a vast sea of heavenly constellation
  coming to berth at earth's harbor
  a garden of myriad dreams,
  there, the purpose of own breath we ponder;

and as we gaze around paradise
  enchanted by its amazing beauty –
  great symmetry of tangling forms
  expressive of divine norms,
  it dawns, that there's always a twin in every speck
  and the soul is lonely without its second fleck;

then we twirl in the dance of desire
  pining for a soulmate –
  the flame of our sailing fire,
  a hand to cushion the rough edges
  of a long an arduous journey,
  over the horizon, a knight in shining armour prowls,
  a heart beckons, another reckons;
  entwined, there's a sweet song of emotion
  in the hollow of strange absurdities,
  twin hearts palpating as one;
  the rhythm inundates a never ending bliss,
  no dark spots but a brilliant hue
  of fused ideas: the bells begin to toll;

a gaily walk on the aisle to the altar,
  hand in hand like the walls of Gibraltar, twin souls
  sturdily deaf to the hues and haas of the world

our future in our tender hands

and the glow in the eyes of our soulmate
the ray that zooms our zeal across time;

and the nuptial knots are tied –
  two varied halves in one genial whole,
  exuberant Siamese smiling in rustling wind,
  we hope to anchor on a future that'll not grind,
  but there comes the test of our will;
  inevitably we stumble, and stumble,
  then we garner strength to move on, and on;

there's a long an arduous journey ahead,
  patience and tolerance to every stead;
  no matter the vagary of emotion
  willed we are not to be punched by time,
  through hills and frills, our reel goes
  and our kind will sprout, so sprout
  from our fusion to tell the warm story.

Oh, Little Faery!

Fair little faery,
   Live not forever at the fringes of my world,
   Nor on the crest of distant dreams -
   Reach out and coax me up into your realms,
   Extend your tenderness and encircle my being,
   Never phase away like vagrant wind
   Come, oh little faery, I bid you stay
   Enter the labyrinth of my heart, express your play.

Only a gentle faery like you could
   Make me swim towards a shimmering buoy
   Out in the roiling sea of emotion
   Without dread of heart wrenching monsters
   Underneath the sea's superficial calm;
   None could contrive images to loom and strengthen
   My resolve for a safe anchor
   In the swirl of world vastly unknown till you reared.

Uregwu

From the cackle of your lips
   Comes the drone of heavenly harp

From the gentle swagger of your hips
   Rears the works of a great sculptor

From the staccato beat of your heart
   sprinkled is the realm
   with the wine of cupid
   from the gods
   eternal toast of a soul to another

With the light of your emerald eyes
   A soul's darkness is banished
   And lost hope once again restored

With the radiance of your smile
   The sun is unleashed at dawn

Wings Of The Mind

Oh gate of a gilded heart
   why do you cringe suddenly ajar
   in submission to cupid's proud dart
   that flung me wondrously afar?
   Why the splurge of this infernal wave
   deep in the shades of the heart's cave
   that resounds with such a high octave?

Oh tender wings of the mind
   must you flutter over every plain
   on the rough crest of passion's swift wind
   in hope that you'll splash in new rain?
   Why is yours a vague and fruitless search
   when there's a stout branch to perch
   which truly is not out of reach?

Oh strange music of the heart
   you trump so sweet a note
   and my resolve is sold from the start
   but how come this stubborn mote
   that threatens to blurt the fantasy of the mind
   a denial of this great ecstasy I find
   in the giddy choice betwixt two a kind?

Oh beautiful gate of my centre
   your glittering frames you can't shut any longer
   enough room you've made for someone to enter
   and the feeling can only get stronger.
   Even if I try so hard to withhold
   what already has been readily told
   it's just another game at being bold.

Desire

from the burrows of heart so tender
   your pebble encroached on my wholesome sea,
   stirred from the honeycomb a romance
   to which ripples of emotions rendered a dance,
   my body, eclipsed with the earthquake tickle
   fire of desire arrested my mind in a manner so fickle;

your scythes, so menacing, unforgiving
   tumbled my ladder of consciousness
   into the abyss of confusion,
   and lurking monsters made smithereens of my bliss,
   a pantheon of love wrecked in mock living;
   oh desire, your macabre dance cut my pinions
   at the peak of an epic cosmic reunion;

the dames – purveyors of your mischief
   nature's gifts they flaunt with unparalleled dexterity,
   their charades: a wink, a wiggle, a smile;
   your impudence I rebuke with a wave of the hand
   but vehement hypnosis I got with your magic wand,
   desire – so cunning is your game of tame;

you make me renege on a vow of transcendence
   oh, how I loathe your transience
   i yearn to be permanently immersed in bliss
   elusive it is unless desire you let me be;
   stupor of your vision I seek divorce
   on reality's wings I'll like to soar so I could see…

providence crowned mw with a dream to nurture
   its charms fetched from the jewel of my true nature,
   effervescent energy that bubbles into the future,
   as oars of eternity, I must row across turbulent Maya

DESIRE

on the surf of time, to rekindle within the shine
hence, a destiny found, and without your huge fine.

Silhouette

SILHOUETTE

And there she was a constant silhouette
   Propped up by happenstance in sweet imagination,
   An exotic flower yet to be truly discovered,
   Scent of her rarity ooze forth bathing the senses
   Like sweet pollen in love's spruce fields,
   But she's a butterfly enflight, askance
   Her mysterious make no one knows
   Enough to try to perch wholly on,
   So she remained a strange silhouette
   In the burst of merry thought.

But only for a while -
   Reality soon took her tender profile
   And vivid the colours that float across;
   She came alive, no longer a silhouette
   Stood like beautifully animated dross
   Her lips cracked into a baleful smile
   The heart huffs sensing her human wile
   Thus vulnerable to cupid's dart
   And attuned too to my shrill jocular.

And then the stir
   Like a snail's languid crawl
   More vigorous with every feigned grin,
   Embracing warm rays like a sunflower
   The silhouette is released to passion,
   Feel her pulse resonate in a new fashion;
   Pains are strummed in the veins to a song
   Images assail the mind like a shrill gong
   Calling for a confluence of hearts
   That we really know ought to be.

Bomadi

BOMADI

Bomadi
   nudged by the inflection of your name
   i watched from your proud shoreline
   the shuttling drafts of your morn tide

hyacinths
   on the murky expanse of water
   bob to carousing whine of engine boats
   hurtling eddies to a perpetual gyration

sand
   of great promontory rose steeply, richly
   across rippling sensations of steady currents
   accommodating the hapless thaw of a people

Bomadi
   though subtle is your seaward breeze
   and idyllic the scenic portraits of your rain forest
   my thoughts are the flotsam of your tide

there
   i'm scurrying on the placid benevolence of water
   edging slowly close to the parapet of oblivion
   drafted easily by the force of fierce yearning

entangled
   listlessly in the numbing mesh of stirring pain
   while wriggling at the vague depths of affection
   my mindset is darned from a precarious web

plodding
   on gossamer thin threads of hazy desire
   the spurn of half-wits, but sheared of profound vision

i wobble along, an ardently proud twerp

goaded
   sheepishly on the devious reins of impulse
   blind like a bat in the tingle of daylight rays
   weaned on by the false thang of love

Bomadi
   the dance of eddies and flotsam of your shores
   are the echoes of myriad lessons
   that love's like the swift current of your ebb and tide

resounding
   always towards the field of total influence
   love's beauteous cascade and huge drafts
   are the beguiling voices of material tide

else
   why do I berth so near, yet far from love's golden shores
   knowing soon your lapping surfs and sensuous tease
   will be drafted away by the strong wave of affluence?

Bomadi
   you failed to warn me in your whispering sweet wind
   of the high stake auction I was ensconced in
   yet you jeer at my squirting tears in your windsong

and how
   do you suppose I would've emerged unscathed
   disparaged and outclassed in the sublime bidding
   by the sheer clout of mundane persuasion?

Flower Of My Dream

Tender flower like a mystic figure sprouts,
   At last alone in the expanse of love;
   A sight that enchants and lures and routs;
   Thrilling magic from above.

She smiles the smile of a genie,
   Buoyed by the radiant petals of compassion;
   Her tawny supple skin like the colours of a genie,
   Flower that invokes intrinsic passion.

The tall flower like some light glows,
   Thrills the dark corners of the heart;
   She's soft and gentle as she flows,
   Mysterious wind that doubles the speed of my cart.

She once sauntered close with her scent,
   Beautiful flower of my dream;
   Her gait forever dainty; each step like a saint,
   That has come to manifest my dream.

Nestled in the comfort of another stage,
   Flower of my dream only perfumes my world;
   But dreams and feels the magic of this stage,
   And a longing heart that waits in my world.

About the Author

Edentu D. Oroso is the head of Special Projects Group for **Kakaaki Magazine**, a magazine published in Nigeria delving into development journalism. He is a seasoned magazine columnist, biographer, motivational speaker, and poet.

A former President of the **Writers' League Benue State University** Makurdi, Edentu is a member of the **Association of Nigerian Authors (ANA) Benue State Chapte**r and its former Director of Welfare.

His published works include the eBook Tears From A Rose, **Wings of Freedom** – a biography of Ralph Igbago; and **The Alfa Sky**, a biography of Air Marshall Ibrahim Mahmud Alfa, Nigeria's longest serving Chief of Air Staff.

He coauthored **The Hidden Treasure** a compendium of essays on former President Goodluck Ebele Jonathan, and coedited **Voice of the Earth**, an anthology of poems. He has been featured in many poetry anthologies such **Sentinel Online**, **Bridge for Birds**, and **Cerebra(lity)**.

You can connect with me on:
- https://www.melodicrosepublishing.com
- https://twitter.com/eoroso
- https://www.facebook.com/edentuoroso
- https://sites.google.com/view/titan-race-novel
- https://sites.google.com/view/strides-of-destiny

Also by Edentu D. Oroso

Titan Race

Twenty-five millennia after he destroyed Atlantis in a fit of fury, Netu Deo, now a Guardian of the modern world, faces a great challenge: Redress his mistake that brought doom to Atlantis and help in the genesis of a new human race – the TITAN RACE.

Guardians of the Blackhole join forces to establish a new civilisation, but find that Netu has called their bluff: His heart reels towards love, disrupting their plan.

The denizens of Atlantis are restless in their quest of vengeance and the modern world hangs on the brink of complete collapse. The fate of all that exists lies in the choices the Guardians and Netu will be forced to make in this intense tale of wit, gut, and sorcery

Strides Of Destiny

STRIDES OF DESTINY is the story of ABBA KYARI - that exceptional super cop. An extraordinary character in the throes of an epoch to cleanse society of social miscreants. In one aspect Strides Of Destiny can read like the ultimate crime thriller. A single vigilante superhero manages to unmask the darkness. His eyes penetrating the recesses of evil and bringing even the strongest villains to their feet. Boko Haram, The Vampire, Godogodo, Evans. These are just some of the criminal organizations and criminals he has brought to the feet of the law. But it is more than that. Strides Of Destiny is the story of a man whose entire existence exudes with integrity and honour. With a strong sense of conviction, Abba Kyari's life leaps off of the page and into your heart. STRIDES OF DESTINY is sure to resonate with you, long after the final page is turned.

www.ingramcontent.com/pod-product-compliance
Lightning Source LLC
Chambersburg PA
CBHW022114040426
42450CB00006B/704